A Painful History of Crime

Lawmakers and the Police

John Townsend

www.raintreepublishers.co.uk

Visit our website to find out more information about **Raintree** books.

To order:
- ☎ Phone 44 (0) 1865 888113
- 🗎 Send a fax to 44 (0) 1865 314091
- 🖥 Visit the Raintree bookshop at **www.raintreepublishers.co.uk** to browse our catalogue and order online.

First published in Great Britain by Raintree, Halley Court, Jordan Hill, Oxford OX2 8EJ, part of Harcourt Education.
Raintree is a registered trademark of Harcourt Education Ltd.

© Harcourt Education Ltd 2005
The moral right of the proprietor has been asserted.

Editorial: Melanie Copland
and Kate Buckingham
Design: Lucy Owen
and Bridge Creative Services Ltd
Picture Research: Hannah Taylor
and Ginny Stroud-Lewis
Production: Duncan Gilbert

Originated by Chroma Graphics (Overseas) Pte. Ltd
Printed and bound in China by South China Printing Company

ISBN 1 844 21390 0
09 08 07 06 05
10 9 8 7 6 5 4 3 2 1

British Library Cataloguing in Publication Data

Townsend, John
Law makers and the police – (A Painful History of Crime)
363.2'09
A full catalogue record for this book is available from the British Library.

Acknowledgements
Alamy Images pp **13t**; **16l** (Alex Segre), **33** (John Angerson), **9** (Mike Hill), **43b** (Oote Boe), Corbis pp **34-35**; **1**, **4**, **6l**, **29** (Royalty Free), **32-33** (James Leynse), **10-11**, **13b**, **25**, **30** (Bettmann), **40** (Douglas Kirkland), **23** (Francis G. Mayer), **42** (Reuters), **4-5** (Sandy Felsenthal), **35** (Underwood & Underwood), Getty Images pp **38** (Photodisc), **41** (The Image Bank), **12**, **21** (Hulton Archive), **10** (Stone), **8-9** (Time & Life Pictures), Mary Evans Picture Library pp **7**, **15**, **17**; **18** (Reproduction of a woodcut from the Bagford Collection, held in The British Museum), Peter Newark Picture Library pp **5m**, **16r**, **22-23**, **24**, **31t**, Photolibrary.com **40-41**, Rex Features **36**, The Ancient Art and Architecture Collection **8**, **11**, The Bridgeman Art Library pp **19** (Peabody Essex Museum, Salem, Massachusetts, USA), **20** (Guildhall Library, Corporation of London, UK), **14** (Private Collection), The Kobal Collection pp **43t** (20th Century Fox), **28** (20th Century Fox/Jurgen Vollmer), **27** (MGM), **24-25** (Miramax/Dimension Films/Chris Large), **26-27** (Morgan Creek/Van Redin), **5t**, **6r** (Paramount/Bud Fraker), **5b**, **31b** (Warner Brothers), The Library of Congress **22t**.

Cover photograph of gavel reproduced with permission of Corbis/Chris Collins.

Every effort has been made to contact copyright holders of any material reproduced in this book. Any omissions will be rectified in subsequent printings if notice is given to the publishers.

The paper used to print this book comes from sustainable resources.

Disclaimer

Contents

Any words appearing in the text in bold,
like this, are explained in the glossary. You can
also look out for them in the Word bank box
at the bottom of each page.

You must not do that!

Laws are made from sets of rules and they tell us all how to behave. They say what is allowed and what is not. The government of a country makes its laws. Police, and the threat of punishment, **enforce** the law.

If we had no rules we could do just what we like. Life would be great … or would it?

- If we had no rules, how would a football match work?
- If we had no rules, how would people drive on the roads?
- If we had no rules, anyone could come into your room and take what they liked.

No one likes to be told, "You must not do that." But often it is for our own good. If we ignore certain rules, we could put ourselves, and others, in danger.

❖ The Capitol Building in Washington, United States, where laws are made.

4   *Word bank*   **enforce**   carry out
guilty   having done wrong

Keeping to the rules

Thousands of years ago, people began to live together in groups. To stop arguments and to make life run smoothly, they made up rules to live by. The same is true today. Each country decides what its laws are and what happens to people who break them. Anyone who breaks the law is committing a crime and becomes a criminal. Once criminals are caught, they are given a **trial** where:

- the case against them is heard
- they have the chance to defend themselves.

If they are found to be **guilty** of the crime, criminals are usually **punished**.

Find out later...

Who made some of the first laws?

Without rules and laws driving through town would be difficult and dangerous.

Who tried to make sure people kept the laws?

Who were some famous law-breakers?

punish   cause pain, suffering, or discomfort for having done wrong

Earliest laws

An eye for an eye

The saying "an eye for an eye and a tooth for a tooth" came from about 3,700 years ago. Moses used it to show that a punishment should match the crime. If someone did something wrong, they should be punished by having the same thing done to them.

All **ancient** people had laws of some kind. Even if they were not written down, laws were passed on so that everyone knew right from wrong.

- The rulers of Egypt made some of the first rules over 4,000 years ago.
- Almost as long ago, King Hammurabi of Babylon had laws written down so people could learn them.
- In about 1300 BC Moses gave the people of ancient Israel ten laws. These were called the ten commandments. They were carved into slabs of stone.

···▶ The story of Moses was told in the 1956 movie *The Ten Commandments*

Word bank   ancient   from a time thousands of years ago

Greeks

Three thousand years ago the ancient Greeks had no clear set of laws or **punishments**. If a person were murdered, their family would find and kill the murderer. This often ended in even more killings.

A way was needed to find if people were **guilty** of a crime or not. So the Greeks set up courts. A court had two "law men". One argued that a crime had been committed and the other argued that it had not. The crowd would then vote for one side or the other. The result was "guilty" or "not guilty". This started the **jury** system that most countries now use today.

Lawmaker

Over 2,500 years ago Draco was one of the first people to write down the laws of Greece. Many of these laws were very strict. Sometimes people who broke the laws were sent away to another country and never allowed back.

❖ A painting of the Areopagus (the rocky hill on the left) where the Greek god Ares stood trial for murder.

jury   group of people that listens to the facts of a case and decides who is guilty

The Romans

About 2,500 years ago the Romans made laws that would bring death to people who broke them. But if you were a rich slave owner, you were more likely to be let off!

The laws were carved into twelve stone slabs and called the Twelve Tables. They stated that people could be put to death if they:
- wrote insulting songs
- cut down a farmer's crops
- burned a stack of corn near a house
- made a noise at night in the city
- stole someone's slave.

The Romans first had the idea that **accused** people were **innocent** until they could be proved **guilty**.

India

About 2,000 years ago, the Laws of Manu were written down in India. Some of the rules were about keeping clean and how to go about life each day. **Priests** have taught these laws for hundreds of years.

This painting shows Indian ladies keeping clean and following the Laws of Manu.

Word bank

accuse   charge with a crime
innocent   not guilty

Beliefs

Religions teach about what is right and wrong. Many of our laws today have come from different religions through time. The prophet Muhammed lived over 1,500 years ago. His teachings were written down in the **Koran**. This was the start of many Islamic laws.

The **Sharia** contains rules that many **Muslims** try to live by. Some of the serious crimes and punishments developed from the Sharia were:

Theft	Right hand cut off (second offence: left foot cut off).
Robbery (theft with violence)	Death by stoning, prison, or right hand cut off.
Drinking wine	80 lashes from a whip, caning, or prison.

In some courts in Iran, laws like this still exist.

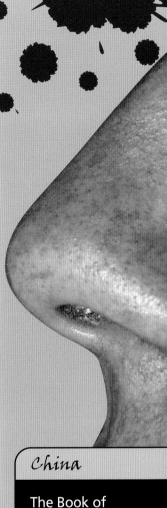

Roman people celebrate while criminals are punished.

China

The Book of Punishments was a book of laws used in China over 2,500 years ago. It set down the ways people were to be punished for serious crimes. Criminals could be tattooed, have their nose cut off, feet cut off, or be put to death. Quite a choice!

Muslim   someone who believes in the religion of Islam and who follows the teachings of Mohammed

Breaking laws

A thousand years ago, countries in Europe had a painful way of finding out if someone was **guilty** of breaking the law. If the jury could not make up its mind, a short test was used. It was called "trial by **ordeal**". This was bad news for the person on trial. He or she had to pick up a lump of red-hot iron, keep hold of it and walk nine paces. The blistered hand was bandaged for three days. After that, if the wound was healing well, it was a sign the person was **innocent**. If not, they were guilty and had to be **punished**.

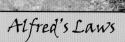

Alfred's Laws

Laws of King Alfred of England (871–899AD):

- If a man lets a tree fall on someone and kill him, the tree must be given to the dead man's family.

- If anyone steals anything in church he is to pay a fine and have his hand cut off.

An illustration of a woman who has been told to walk over hot coals to prove her innocence.

Word bank   ordeal   painful or stressful experience

Aztec law

The Aztec people lived in Mexico nearly 900 years ago. They had some harsh punishments for anyone who broke their laws. They had courts with judges who listened to each case and decided what should happen. Any sort of theft was seen as serious. Homes had no doors that locked, so people trusted each other not to steal. Theft was rare.

If people were found guilty of stealing from stalls in markets, they would be strangled to death. People guilty of dealing in stolen goods could be beaten or have their home knocked down. It could even mean becoming a slave to the person they stole from.

The Incas

Between 1200 and 1535, the Inca people (below) lived in part of South America. Crime was rare. Criminals and their families would be put to death to make sure it stayed that way. Even lying was seen as a crime so Incas always told the truth!

Old Europe

In 1066 the Normans from France invaded England. For killing a Norman soldier, an English person could be fined £30. If they did not **confess** to the murder, the whole of their village had to put all their money together to pay the fine!

Laws in England 900 years ago were very different from laws today. It was the time we now call the **Middle Ages**. The law then was unfair, especially for women. The Church saw men as more important and the law followed this idea. These were some of the laws affecting women:

- no woman could travel on her own
- when a woman married, all her jewels and clothes belonged to her husband
- a man could divorce his wife, but a wife could never divorce her husband
- only women could be **accused** of nagging. They could be ducked in the river for such a crime.

The story of the Norman takeover of England was told in the Bayeaux Tapestry, a giant embroidered cloth.

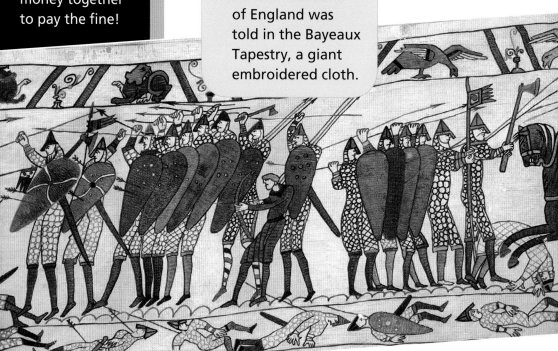

Word bank

baron   person of great power or influence
confess   own up to doing something wrong

Signed and sealed

Kings of England had the power to make the laws. Rich **barons** also had a hand in some lawmaking. King John was a cruel king who wanted greater power. His barons were worried by this and drew up a list of laws they wanted him to agree to. He finally signed these 63 basic rights, such as:

- no one is to go to prison without a **trial**
- **taxes** must be fair
- all people can travel where they like.

These laws and many others in the **Magna Carta** of 1215 have lasted hundreds of years.

The Magna Carta.

Hanging

Most towns in the Middle Ages had a **gallows**. People were hung on these and their bodies left to rot as a warning to others. In 1202, the city of Lincoln, UK had 114 murders, 89 robberies, and 65 people were hurt in fights. Yet only two people were hanged – so many criminals must have got away with their crimes.

gallows wooden frame from which criminals were hanged
tax charge set by leaders or government to pay for public services

13

Life was hard in Europe during the **Middle Ages**. There was a lot of fear about. People were scared about **plagues** and other diseases. They were scared about witches. Beggars also scared them. That was why laws were made to make it easier to kill anyone thought to be a witch or a beggar.

Tramps

Across Europe in the 1500s, rich people were getting richer by **trading** more and more. But poor people were getting even poorer. Higher **taxes**, fewer jobs, and more wars meant many of the poor lost their homes.

In England this made a lot of the rich landowners worried. They feared that the poor would turn to crime. They thought that those who did not work were lazy and wicked. Tramps were seen as a threat. To protect people from "the evil poor", new strict laws were brought in.

> "All parts of England and Wales are pestered with **vagrants** and beggars who commit murders, thefts, and other outrages."
>
> *(From a law in 1572.)*

An illustration from 1567 shows a beggar being led through the streets and whipped.

Word bank   **plague**   deadly disease that spreads quickly over a large area

A crime to be poor

Tramps and beggars with no home or job wandered through Europe. Some villages tried to help their own poor, but travelling vagrants were not so welcome. In some countries, vagrants were pests. In others they were criminals. By 1594 there were around 12,000 beggars in London alone.

"Every person found begging is to be stripped naked from the middle upwards and whipped, until his or her body is bloody. They will then be sent to their birthplace. If they do not know where this is, they will be sent to prison for a year unless someone gives them a job."

(An English law from 1598.)

This illustration shows a tramp, tied to a cart, being whipped.

Laws to deal with vagrants

1547: First vagrancy offence = 2 years slavery. Second offence = slave for life or **execution**. Branded with a "V" on their faces.

1572: First vagrancy offence = whipping and burning of an ear.

1598: Vagrants to be whipped and sent home, sent abroad or executed.

1601: The Poor Law makes villages pay to look after their own vagrants.

trading   buying and selling goods to make money
vagrant   person who has no steady job and wanders from place to place

Catching criminals

No country had a police force over 300 years ago. So who caught the lawbreakers? In England, the job of fighting crime fell to ordinary people.

All men over 12 years old had to belong to a group of 10 called a **tithing**. If somebody robbed you, or if you saw a crime, it was up to you to tell your tithing. It also meant shouting to tell everyone. This was called raising the **hue and cry**. Everybody then ran to help. If they caught someone, they made an **arrest**. If the criminal put up a fight, people were even allowed to kill him or her. No police were needed!

⠿ Anyone found guilty of **heresy** could be burned to death.

Word bank **hue and cry** loud shout once used when chasing a criminal

The Bloody Code

In the 1600s English towns were growing larger. With more people, but no police about, crime rates began to rise. Lawmakers had to get tough, so they kept making new laws. Anyone who broke them could be put to death, often by being hanged in public. This was called "The Bloody Code".

In 1660 the number of crimes with the death **penalty** was about 50. This grew to 288 in the late 1700s. You could be hanged for stealing from a shipwreck or cutting down a young tree. If a woman killed her husband, she would be burned at the stake in front of crowds of people.

tithing   groups of 10 men who were responsible for each other's behaviour

Police on the scene

Crime arrives in America

In the 1600s, Europeans arrived in North America and began to set up small towns. Crime soon followed!

1620: The "Pilgrim Fathers" of England arrived in Massachusetts in the ship *The Mayflower*.

1630s: The first watchmen began to patrol the first towns at night to protect homes from robbers.

Before the 1700s, there was no such thing as an organized, paid police force anywhere. Solving crime and catching criminals was still up to ordinary people. Since Roman times, people have paid guards to protect them and their property. As towns began to grow, they started to pay men to keep a watch on streets at night. They were called "watchmen".

In 1636 the city of Boston in the United States set up its first "Night Watch". New York City started the "Shout and Rattle Watch" in 1651. As soon as watchmen came across trouble they had to shout and shake a wooden rattle to call for help.

•••➔ A painting of the Pilgrim Fathers arriving in America.

Word bank   **illegal**   against the law

Charleys

Watchmen in London, England, were called Charleys after the king at the time: King Charles II. House owners had to pay the men to guard their street at night. But a crime wave in 1728 meant that the watchmen needed to do more than just keep watch.

"Let each Watchman be given a trumpet to sound an alarm in time of danger. It will be **illegal** for anyone else to sound a trumpet in the city. So the Watchmen can see well, lamps will be set up in the street. These will prevent more robberies."

(Weekly Journal, 5th October 1728.)

Bad job

The first American watchmen were given the nickname "leather heads". This was because of their leather hats, but also because they were not thought to be very clever. Many people thought being a watchman was a terrible job. Sometimes criminals were even made to become watchmen as a **punishment**!

An illustration of a night watchman patrolling the streets with his dog.

19

Rising crime

Through the 1700s in Europe and the United States, the policing of towns and cities did not change much. Part-time constables and watchmen kept an eye on villages and towns. But cities were growing fast. There were no organized teams of "crime fighters" so crime in some places was becoming more common.

In London, the Charleys had no power and were seen as useless. They spent most of their time playing cards or sleeping. Some of them took **bribes** from criminals, so they even helped crime rather than stopping it! City leaders were worried. Something had to be done, or crime would get out of control.

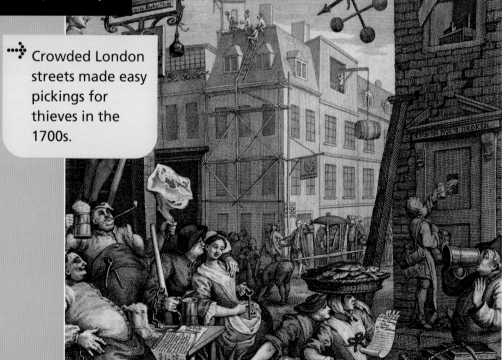

••• Crowded London streets made easy pickings for thieves in the 1700s.

Word bank   **bribe**   payment given to someone to make them act dishonestly

Bow Street Runners

In the 1750s, the big cities of the world were only the size of today's towns. London had half a million people. It would take New York another 100 years to reach that size. Even so, cities were getting too big to cope with crime. Half a million people crammed in crowded streets made easy pickings for criminals.

A man called Henry Fielding in London said it was time to act. He made plans to control crime by turning his house into a base for constables. It became the first police station – in Bow Street. His first team of officers was called "The Bow Street Runners".

The first police in the world

1750s: London's Bow Street Runners become the first small group of paid policemen.

1830s: The first police forces begin in Australia.

1850s: The first police forces begin in the United States.

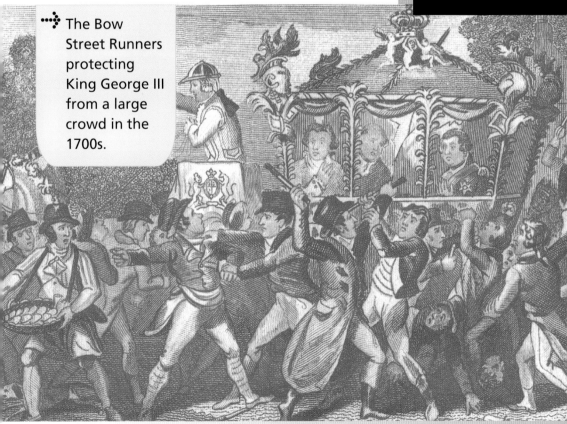

The Bow Street Runners protecting King George III from a large crowd in the 1700s.

volunteer   someone who offers to do a job without payment

Land of the free

The laws of every country have grown and changed over hundreds of years. Lawmakers have had to make new laws clear to everyone. This was important in the United States, which began to rule itself in 1783. Before then, the UK made the United States' laws.

The new US "law book" was called The **Constitution**. George Washington, the first US president, signed it in 1787. Since then there have been hundreds of changes to it. This is still the "law of the land" that all US police officers have to uphold.

Just for the record

The US Constitution was written in Independence Hall (above), which still stands today in Philadelphia. This set of laws was written in secret, behind locked doors. The first ten **amendments** were added in 1791. These became known as The Bill of Rights.

Word bank   amendment   change in wording or meaning
constitution   basic beliefs and laws of a nation

Angry mob

The new law in the United States was soon broken. In the 1790s, farmers in Pennsylvania were so angry about a new **tax** that they began to **riot**. They smashed up towns and beat tax collectors. A mob attacked a **marshal** in Allegheny County in 1794, and several hundred men burned down a tax inspector's home. The government had to act. As there was no police force, President Washington called out the army. About 13,000 soldiers had to restore law and order.

American soldiers controlling the mob in Pennsylvania in 1794.

Keeping the peace

The riots of the 1790s were a great test for the new US government and its laws. Soldiers **arrested** only about twelve men, who went on **trial** in Philadelphia. President Washington (below) chose to release them. He had proved his point that soldiers could be used to **enforce** the law.

---

marshal officer of the government, similar to a sheriff
riot cause public violence and disorder

23

Peelers and Rangers

Robert Peel was a member of the UK Government. In 1828 he looked into the crime problems of London. He saw how the police were poorly run, and only part-time. He set up plans to organize them better. They needed to be full-time, **professional** officers.

The next year, the Metropolitan Police Force began. There were 3,200 men employed to look after the centre of London. Many people were pleased to see them and called them "Bobbies" or "Peelers" after Robert Peel. Like today's police officers, their job was mainly:

- to prevent crime
- to find criminals
- to protect life and property
- to keep the peace.

Word bank   **gold rush**   time when workers flood into an area to dig for gold

First US cops

News of the new London police force spread to other countries. In a few years, other paid police forces started across the world. The Texas Rangers began as a small group of **volunteers** who tried to catch criminals. From 1835 they were paid, and were some of the first full-time police officers in the United States. They were tough – they were known for being heavy-handed and "shooting first and asking questions later".

In California the **gold rush** of 1848 brought so many rowdy gold diggers that more police had to be found. Soon police forces grew all across the United States, becoming organized and better at catching the lawbreakers.

US police tackle a gang of cotton thieves.

The 2001 movie *The Texas Rangers* showed the life of the early lawmen.

Getting started

1850: New York has half a million people and an organized police force.

1853: Los Angeles Police Department begins.

1856: Philadelphia has a quarter of a million people and a police force.

1859: Boston Police Force begins.

professional   working in a full-time paid job
truncheon   police officer's wooden stick or club

Crime fighters

Lawbreakers have been around for hundreds of years. Lawmakers and crime fighters have always tried to keep ahead of the criminals. Sometimes it seemed as if criminals were winning the fight.

Outlaws

At different times in history, outlaws seemed to do very well. They went around ignoring the law. As they lived "outside the law" they were called "outlaws".

One of the main times for outlaws in the United States was in the late 1800s when people began to move west across the country. Many small towns sprung up where gold was found.

Lawbreakers shot by the lawmakers

Billy the Kid aged 21: shot dead in 1881 by Pat Garrett.

Jesse James aged 34: shot in 1882 by Robert Ford.

Bill Doolin aged 38: shot dead in 1896 by a **marshal**.

···▶ Banks, **stagecoaches**, and the railroad became targets for outlaws in the Wild West. This is from the 2001 movie *American Outlaws*.

Word bank **stagecoach** wagon pulled by horses from town to town

Wanted

In the Wild West there was a lot of fighting between outlaws and the Native Americans. Guns, wild country to hide in, and few police meant that outlaws could escape getting caught.

Sheriffs had the job of tracking down outlaws. But some of the sheriffs seemed to act like criminals themselves. A few of them shot first and asked questions later. That made life dangerous for everyone. Wild West towns had "wanted" posters offering rewards to anyone who could catch outlaws – dead or alive.

Lawman

Pat Garrett was a bartender in the Wild West before becoming a sheriff in Lincoln County, New Mexico. Apart from hunting down the famous outlaw Billy the Kid, he became a captain of the Texas Rangers. Garrett was killed by the gunman Jim Miller in 1908.

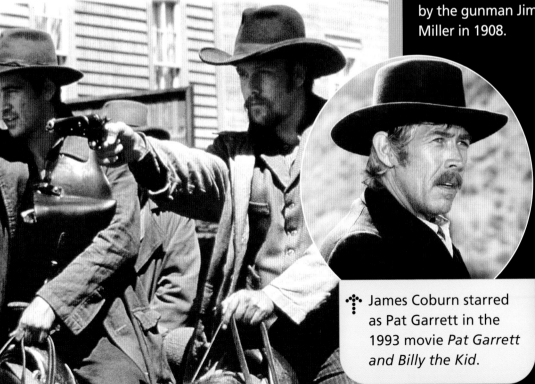

James Coburn starred as Pat Garrett in the 1993 movie *Pat Garrett and Billy the Kid.*

In 1875, London's police headquarters opened at Great Scotland Yard. Now called New Scotland Yard, it is responsible for the police work of Greater London. London police are sometimes called "Yardies" after the name of their head office.

Murder on the streets

Murder has always been against the law in most places. Sometimes a murderer strikes a number of times for what seems like no reason. People panic and the police are under great pressure to track down the **serial killer.**

The 2001 movie *From Hell* told the gruesome story of Jack the Ripper.

Word bank   **forensic test**   scientific investigation to help solve a crime

Mystery

By the end of the 1800s, London had 7 million people, so crimes had to be solved all the time. But the 16,000 policemen of the city were just not ready for a serial killer. During 1888 five women were found dead in the dark streets.

Jack the Ripper

At that time, there were no police scientists to carry out detailed **forensic tests** on the victims. the only clue they had was a letter sent to them, from someone claiming to be the killer. The letter was signed "Jack the Ripper". More letters followed.

The investigation into the murders was led by Inspector Frederick Abberline. He had many police detectives working on the murder cases. They worked hard at solving the murders, and even named a few suspects. However none of these was ever charged.

After all their work the police still had no real clues to go on. Many people began to question the police and eventually the head of the police resigned. Then the murders suddenly stopped. The mystery was never solved.

The killer

Was one of the most famous lawbreakers of all time a doctor? Many of the police working on the Jack the Ripper murders thought the killer must have been a medical expert. His work with the **scalpel** showed great skill ... and horror.

---

scalpel   knife with a small sharp blade used by a surgeon
serial killer   murderer who kills more than once over a period of time

...ghteenth
...ment of the
...stitution was:

...aking,
... or carrying
...hol in the
...States is
...ited."

...w lasted
...rs. It
...nother
...ment to stop
...v in 1933.

Gangsters

The 1920s and 1930s were hard times in many cities across the world. There were not enough jobs or money. In 1929 hundreds of businesses failed in New York. This led to the Depression, when many people lost their jobs and all their money. Some of them turned to crime to make a living.

Also in the 1920s, the United States made a law to stop drunken mobs causing trouble in the streets. It banned alcohol. Now it was **illegal** to make or sell such drinks. This led to whisky smuggling and a wave of organized crime. Parts of New York were in the grip of violent gangsters.

...the 1920s, all
...cohol in the
...nited States
...ad to be
...oured away.

Bonnie and Clyde

The Texas Rangers had to deal with some of the gangster crime of the 1930s. A couple of bank robbers called Bonnie Parker and Clyde Barrow had shot people in Texas. Frank Hamer was a Texas Ranger with the job of trying to "break the lawbreakers". He hunted for Bonnie and Clyde for 102 days. With other rangers, he finally caught up with them in Louisiana. He hoped to take them alive, but they reached for their guns. Hamer and his men fired. Bonnie and Clyde died in a hail of bullets in 1934.

Clyde's car, full of bullet holes after the police shooting.

The movie *Bonnie and Clyde* was made in 1967.

Organized crime

Police in some US cities had to deal with gangs robbing banks with machine guns before they sped off in getaway cars. The only trouble was, a few of the police at that time were also criminals. They could sometimes be **bribed** to let the gangsters escape!

Most wanted

For nearly 100 years a team of crime fighters has been at work across the United States. Today it is called the **FBI** and it tackles some of the most serious crimes. For over 50 years, the FBI has shown the faces of its "most wanted" criminals. It first printed a list of them in 1949 and since then the public have helped to find the lawbreakers.

By putting the list in public places, in newspapers, and on television, the FBI gets a good response from the public. Today, the list appears on the Internet, so the most wanted are seen all over the world in a matter of seconds.

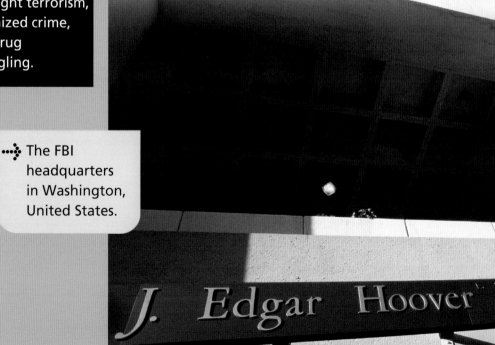

···◊ The FBI headquarters in Washington, United States.

Word bank   FBI   United States' Federal Bureau of Investigation, which investigates serious crime

From car thieves to terrorists

The "most wanted" list has shown how US crime has changed. At first, bank robbers, burglars, and car thieves were the main lawbreakers. In the 1960s, there were more vandals who attacked and damaged government property. More kidnappers were on the list, too. As **organized crime** grew across the world, the list changed again through the 1970s. Today, many of the lawbreakers being hunted are major drug dealers and **terrorists**. We are all asked to become the eyes and ears of the criminal catchers.

Caught on

Television programmes such as America's Most Wanted or the UK's Crimewatch have found many people who keep breaking the law. Having a famous face can soon get you **arrested**!

organized crime   large organizations involved in crimes in many countries
terrorists   political criminals who use violence to get what they want

33

Changing laws

Slave law

Laws change as people's ideas of what is right and wrong change over time. New laws and new crimes mean the police must keep changing, too. Today we can do some things that were once **illegal**. We are also **forbidden** from doing things that were once allowed.

Slaves

Slavery has existed for thousands of years, in countries all over the world. There were once no laws to stop it, or to protect slaves. The UK made a law to stop slavery in 1833. More countries also began to make it illegal. Yet types of slavery still happen in some countries. Two men from Albania were sent to prison in the UK in 2005 for **people-trafficking** and selling people into forced labour.

Slave law

The UK made a law in 1807 to stop ships carrying slaves. But the law did not go far enough. It just meant a captain could be fined for every slave found on his ship. It took another 26 years before slavery became illegal. Slavery became illegal in the United States in 1865 when the thirteenth **amendment** banned it.

When people protest, like during this march in Washington, United States, 1963, laws can be changed.

Word bank   forbidden   not allowed by law

Fighting the law

All through history, ordinary people have had to fight to change unfair laws. Sometimes they used peaceful protests. Sometimes their efforts were violent. In the United States it was once forbidden for:

- women to vote
- anyone to buy or drink alcohol
- black people to go to certain areas.

People protested over time in many ways. Marches, hunger strikes, silent protests, and **riots** have all managed to get laws changed. In 1964 the Civil Rights Act was a new law in the United States. At last no one could be treated differently because of his or her race, colour, or religion.

Police arrest a woman who was protesting about not being able to vote, London, UK, 1914.

Votes for women

For years, women tried to change the law to allow them to vote. Eventually their protests worked:

1918 (UK): women over the age of 30 were finally allowed to vote.

1920 (United States): 19th amendment: "The right of citizens in the US to vote shall not be denied on account of thier sex."

people-trafficking smuggling people into different countries using violence and fear

In 1915 Australia's New South Wales Police Department advertised two jobs for women police officers. Nearly 500 women applied. The two women who got the jobs were the first police women in Australia. They wore their own clothes and had no uniforms.

Enforcing the law

It took years of struggle, protest, and lawbreaking for the law in many countries to treat all people fairly. Some countries are still fighting.

Women were not allowed to join the police force at first. In the United States, the first female police officer was taken on in 1910. Her name was Alice Stebbin Wells. In the UK the first women police officers appeared in 1949. They had to be between 22 and 35 years of age and were not allowed to work on night duty. Today, women work at all levels in police forces around the world and do the same duties as men.

Today Australia has thousands of women police officers.

Word bank   **flying squad**   "rapid response" police unit investigating major crimes

Law enforcers

Today's US police are very different from those in the past. Especially the Los Angeles Police Department (LAPD). Today it is one of the largest police forces in the world. With almost 10,000 police officers, it deals with some of the most serious crime in the United States. In 1940 there were still only about 40 women officers. Today, hundreds of the LAPD officers are women.

Since the LAPD began in 1853, the car has been **invented**. With it came many new traffic laws and traffic police. A **flying squad** with two "automobiles" and two officers joined the LAPD in 1918. Today there are quite a few more!

Traffic police

In the United States today, no one thinks twice when a police motorbike or a squad car patrols the highways in search of lawbreakers on wheels. The LAPD makes more than 500,000 traffic stops per year. Chases happen more often in films and on television shows!

❖••• The LAPD slogan "to protect and to serve" was first used in 1955.

invent   make or discover something for the first time

Global crime

Fast, cheap air travel and computers changed the world. At one time each country looked after its own laws and lawbreakers. Not any more. Criminals can now travel the world in hours. So must the police. Many laws are **international**, too. After all, a criminal can now commit a crime from a computer desk in another country! The Internet has made **cyber crime** a problem across the world.

As long ago as 1923 a special police force was set up to catch criminals who escaped to other countries. It was called Interpol. It is still busy today and works in about 180 countries. Its headquarters are in Lyon, France.

War on terror

The world's police must work together today like never before. Laws have changed in the fight to stop terrorists attacking different countries. Now some countries can put anyone in prison that they suspect of being a terrorist – without a **trial**.

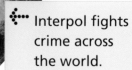

Interpol fights crime across the world.

Word bank   cyber crime   using computers and the Internet to commit a crime

Not so global

Not all laws today are international. Visitors to countries can break laws without knowing it and end up in trouble. It happens every year. Did you know…

- Many countries forbid taking photographs or using binoculars near government buildings. Tourists in Egypt, Greece, and Cuba have ended up in prison after breaking this law.
- It is **illegal** to swear in public in Bahrain, the UAE (United Arab Emirates), and Kenya. You may have to pay a high fine if you are caught.
- In the UAE it is against the law to eat, drink, or smoke in public at certain times.

It pays to know the laws of the land!

Guess what…

In Singapore, dropping litter, **jaywalking**, spitting, feeding birds in public places, chewing gum on the local transport system, and failing to flush public toilets are against the law. Such crimes can get you instant fines.

Pick up your litter or get arrested!

jaywalking   crossing a street carelessly without paying attention to traffic laws

Strange times

Old laws of Ohio

US cities had their own city laws. These are some unusual laws from some Ohio cities:

- Any person found leaning against a public building can be fined.

- It is a crime to eat a doughnut and walk backwards on a city street.

- A policeman may bite a dog to quieten it.

There are many old laws in different countries that must have made sense at the time, but seem a little crazy now! Some old, odd laws that came and went at different times in the United States seem rather strange today:

- You may not swear in front of women and children in the state of Michigan.
- It is illegal to fish for whales on Sunday in Ohio.
- A special law in Florida banned unmarried women from parachuting on Sunday.
- It is **illegal** to sing in a public place while wearing a swimsuit in Florida.

Word bank   **disorderly conduct**   behaving in a rowdy manner that upsets other people

Free speech and the law

Two men were arrested outside a New York court for telling jokes about lawyers.

"How do you tell when a lawyer is lying?" Harvey Kash, 69, said to Carl Lanzisera, 65. "His lips are moving!"

A lawyer standing in front of them was not amused and had them charged with disorderly conduct.

"They put the handcuffs on us, frisked us, sat us down and checked our driver's licenses," Mr Lanzisera said.

A spokesman for the court said the men were causing a stir. "Their First Amendment rights to free speech were affecting the rights of others at the court."

(2005)

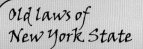

Old laws of New York State

- It is a crime to throw a ball at someone's head for fun.

- It is a crime to put naked dummies on display.

- A licence is needed to use a clothes line outside.

Can you think why there was a law against naked dummies?

41

And finally...

Did you know?

New laws are always being talked about and voted for by **politicians**. In the United States, new laws start out as bills in Congress, the House of Representatives, or the Senate. In the UK and Australia, bills have to be discussed and voted on in the Houses of Parliament before they become law.

We would all like to be able to do whatever we want. But if everyone did just as they wanted, we would all suffer. People who do not respect others or their property have to be made to! Laws stop us all doing many things, but they can also give us greater freedom by making the world safer.

All through history, laws have been made and changed to fit the changing times. Hundreds of new laws were needed when people started to drive cars. Without traffic laws and police to **enforce** them, people would be driving all over the place at great speed! In fact – they often still do!

US lawmakers at work inside the Capitol in Washington.

Word bank   pedestrian   someone who walks along the street

There will always be people who are prepared to break the law. But this story shows that some people break certain laws, but will not break others!

HIGHWAY CODE CATCHES THIEF

A thief who ran from a jewellery shop after stealing a necklace stopped 15 metres (49 feet) down the street. He waited for the lights to change at a **pedestrian** crossing. The shop owner ran after the thief, but was amazed to see him waiting at the lights. The jeweller pulled him to the ground and held on until police came. The police said: "We caught the thief because he didn't want to cross the road **illegally**."

(7th December 2004)

✦ Just another cop movie!

✦ Even some criminals obey traffic laws.

In films

Where would we be without all the lawmakers and the police? Over 5 million people around the world are police officers. There are hundreds more who pretend to be! There are probably more "cop movies" than any other type of film. The world of crime is still big business in the 21st century.

politician   person who takes an active part in party politics or in government business

Find out more

Books

Behind the Scenes: Solving a Crime, Peter Mellet (Heinemann Library, 1999)

Interpol: International Organizations, Jean F. Blashfield (Gareth Stevens, 2003)

Police Officers, Shannon Zemlicka (Lerner Publications, 2004)

True Crime: Cops and Robbers, John Townsend (Raintree, 2005)

Using the Internet

Explore the Internet to find out more about crime through time. You can use a search engine, such as www.yahooligans.com, and type in keywords such as:

- Robert Peel
- criminal
- the Riot Act.

Search tips

There are billions of pages on the Internet so it can be difficult to find exactly what you are looking for.

These search tips will help you find websites more quickly:

- Know exactly what you want to find out about first.
- Use two to six keywords in a search, putting the most important words first.
- Be precise. Only use names of people, places, or things.

Crime Through Time

1215	England	Writing of the Magna Carta (Law of the Land).
1253	England	Parish constables start patrolling some areas, being paid by local residents.
1475	England	**Invention** of the muzzle-loading musket.
1539	England	First criminal court established at Old Bailey.
1718	England	Machine gun invented by James Puckle.
1789	United States	Constitution (Law) **ratified**.
1829	UK	Sir Robert Peel begins a proper police force with 1,000 uniformed police officers, based at Scotland Yard, London.
1830	United States	First revolver made by Samuel Colt.
1833	United States	First paid police force in the United States, based in Philadelphia.
1868	UK	Last public hanging in the UK.
1870	United States	Creation of Department of Justice.
1878	UK	Creation of Criminal Investigation Department.
1935	United States	Bureau of Investigations becomes the Federal Bureau of Investigations (FBI).
1936	United States	Last public hanging.
1987	UK	First use of DNA typing in solving crimes.

Glossary

accuse charge with a crime

amendment change in wording or meaning

ancient from a time thousands of years ago

arrested to be taken in for questioning about a crime

baron person of great power or influence

bribe payment given to someone to make them act dishonestly

confess own up to doing something wrong

constitution basic beliefs and laws of a nation

cyber crime using computers and the Internet to commit a crime

disorderly conduct behaving in a rowdy manner that upsets other people

enforce carry out

execute put to death by law

FBI United States' Federal Bureau of Investigation, which investigates serious crime

flying squad "rapid response" police unit investigating major crimes

forbidden not allowed by law

forensic test scientific investigation to help solve a crime

gallows wooden frame from which criminals were hanged

gold rush time when workers flood into an area to dig for gold

guilty having done wrong

heresy having opposite beliefs to those of a church

hue and cry loud outcry once used when chasing a criminal

illegal against the law

innocent not guilty

international affecting different countries

interpreted taken to mean something

invent make or discover something for the first time

jaywalking crossing a street carelessly without paying attention to traffic laws

jury group of people that listens to the facts of a case and decides who is guilty

Koran holy book of Islam

Magna Carta Law of the Land

marshal officer of the government, similar to a sheriff

Middle Ages period of European history from about 800 to about 1500

Muslim someone who believes in the religion of Islam and who follows the teachings of Mohammed

ordeal painful or stressful experience

organized crime large organizations involved in crimes in many countries

pedestrian someone who walks along the street

penalty punishment given for breaking a rule

people-trafficking smuggling people into different countries using violence and fear

plague deadly disease that spreads quickly over a large area

politician person who takes an active part in party politics or in government business

priest person who performs religious ceremonies

professional working in a full-time paid job

prohibited not allowed by law

punish cause pain, suffering, or discomfort for having done wrong

ratified to be made official

riot cause public violence and disorder

scalpel knife with a small sharp blade used by a surgeon

serial killer murderer who kills more than once over a period of time

Sharia traditional law system of Muslims

sheriff official of a "shire" in charge of enforcing the law

stagecoach wagon pulled by horses from town to town

tax charge set by leaders or government to pay for public services

terrorists political criminals who use violence to get what they want

tithing groups of 10 men who were responsible for each other's behaviour

trading buying and selling goods to make money

trial hearing and judgement of a case in court

truncheon police officer's wooden stick or club

vagrant person who has no steady job and wanders from place to place

volunteer someone who offers to do a job without payment

Index

Titles in the *A Painful History Of Crime* series include:

Crime Through Time

John Townsend

Hardback   1 844 21391 9

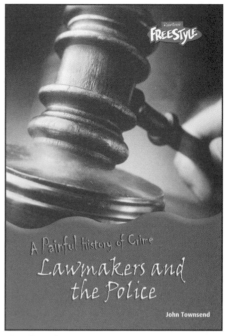

Lawmakers and the Police

John Townsend

Hardback   1 844 21390 0

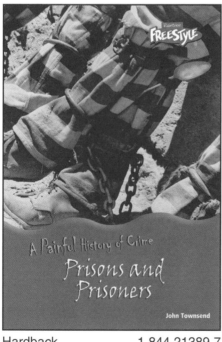

Prisons and Prisoners

John Townsend

Hardback   1 844 21389 7

Punishment and Pain

John Townsend

Hardback   1 844 21388 9

Find out about other titles on our website www.raintreepublishers.co.uk